A

Inside Perceptions of Communication,
Interaction, Thoughts & Feelings

Paul Isaacs

Foreword by Susan Rowling

chipmunkapublishing
the mental health publisher

Published by
Chipmunkapublishing
United Kingdom

http://www.chipmunkapublishing.com

ISBN   978-1-78382-066-5

Chipmunkapublishing gratefully acknowledge the support of Arts Council England.

Chapters

Paul Isaacs

I would like to thank Donna Williams for her constant help, direction and wisdom for people on the spectrum, including myself and the creation of the "Fruit Salad" Analogy (D. Williams 1995, 2005) which has helped me and so many others

Paul Isaacs

Foreword

Before Paul asked me to proofread this book I knew very little about autism, let alone how an autistic person thinks and feels. In this informative book Paul explains just that. He sets out his own thoughts and feelings in a clear and concise manner which is easy to read and digest. Paul gives his personal views on a whole range of subjects including early development, diagnosis, communication, emotions, relationships, education, employment and much more.

Drawing on his own life experiences Paul provides a unique insight which will be invaluable to others on the autism spectrum as well as anyone wishing to have a better understanding of how an autistic person thinks. Paul's honesty is refreshing and, at times, very touching. Paul has truly found his niche in helping others through his work for Autism Oxford.

Thanks to Paul I now have a much better understanding of life from an autistic's perspective.

Susan Rowling

Paul Isaacs

Author Introduction

I became involved in the autism "community" in 2007 after going to a group for people on the spectrum and starting at an autism base as a volunteer for over two years. In between days I began to speak for Autism Oxford, which promotes the awareness of Asperger's Syndrome and Autism within the Oxfordshire and Buckinghamshire area, and I have presented many speeches for Autism Oxford and the NAS which has given me a lot of confidence. I was formally diagnosed in 2010 with Autism & Scotopic Sensitivity Syndrome in 2012 and I work as a Speaker, Trainer, Author and Consultant in and around the UK.

Paul Isaacs

Developmental History, Diagnosis & Autism Oxford

Me in October 1986 © Isaacs Family Photo

I have a different diagnosis to people with Asperger's Syndrome; I have Autism. I have had a different developmental pathway to many people with Asperger's and therefore a different perspective. I would also like to point out that although I have many views they do not reflect the whole autism community, but will give you a glimpse (or more) into what it is like to live on the autism spectrum and hopefully help many people in the process.

My personal take on language was through my senses rather than the verbal comprehension. I was a late talker and didn't begin to talk at functional level until I was 7 or 8 years old. I was severely autistic as a child which is called Classic/Kanner's Autism. I had and still have receptive language problems (meaning deafness). I have many visual agnosias which are a part of my autism (agnosia is neurological "blindness" due to damage to specific brain regions) and object blindness, which means I see things in a fragmented form; not seeing the whole but pieces, colours, shapes and reflections. This means from the onset language in its base verbal form was not apparent to me. My senses were my primary form of language. The use of touch and the information I would get back from touching is this object rough or smooth? Long or short? I think with a sensory train of thought, not verbal logic.

Autism can be a gift for some, for others it can be an unbreakable cage. It's useful to understand that it is a complex mix of ability and disability. It's through understanding both aspects that one broadens not only their understanding of themselves but of other people on the autism spectrum also. Staying positive for me has been a true asset and not feeling sorry for one's self has been key to where I am today. Being empathetic and showing empathy with others has helped. Learning that other people in the world have their own sets of values and forms of morality and understanding, however hard it is, that people have different views to your own.

Sometimes professionals in the field of autism have very narrow minded views of what it is to be autistic and how it affects a person. However, the professional who diagnosed me and my family was very receptive. This proves that there are specialists out in the world who listen to the person, show genuine kindness and treat the person with the respect every human being deserves. I do consider my family and I to be very lucky and it can be seen that specialists like this are what is termed "goldust" (no not the WWE wrestler!), It's a term that is used for people who are rare in their field of work, in this case autism.

Staying true to oneself is the best way forward. Having strong firm foundations to build from is key and also having support networks in times of crisis, which many people on the spectrum experience a lot in their lives, is paramount also.

When I was born I was born a human being and funnily enough I'm still a human being now! As a small child I had severe autism (which means I had autism with a severe learning disability and/or severe sensory and communication difficulties). So I had two things going on in my development; my autism which affected my social skills, sensory perception, imaginative play, emotional recognition (for myself and others) and my ability to be a typical child. The next thing was being learning disabled (now I just have learning difficulties); this affects your global cognitive, emotional and social functioning which was impaired.

The preconceptions of what was "wrong" with me at pre-school came about through idle gossip from teachers and parents and a firm belief that I was being "damaged" emotionally at home. This came through a visit from the head teacher to home wanting to know how I was and observing my homely surroundings. My Mum has said that she was thankful that the teacher didn't get the social services involved to take me away. The issues can arise from people making some very bold assumptions about a child and in this case that was true. How can some people develop more than others and how can some people with autism regress for no apparent reason? The truth of the matter is you are dealing with human beings and much like anybody else in the world they deserve respect, empathy and commitment in order for people on the autism spectrum (wherever they lie on the spectrum) to get the most out of life. They need understanding people around them to thrive and be happy which I think is one of the most impressive and inspiring goals to reach; it's beyond "intelligence" and all the playground red tape that goes with it. Happiness is a sense of contentment which people on the spectrum deserve to feel.

My diagnosis is Autism. I was diagnosed by a man who shows an interest in the disorder but also in the people who have the disorder; that is the key, the holistic pathway of understanding which has helped me and my family. It's about give and take and selflessness and understanding each other. That, I believe, is what makes a brilliant

14

foundation for autistic specific support which I have received from him. And even though he is based in Cardiff which is miles away he still keeps in contact and tries to support me when he can. Amazing is all I can say!

Within Autism (a developmental disability) there are strong islets of ability. I have a deep memory (savant like) in my knowledge of autism and all the technical names for the processing disorders that come with it. I have a good memory for dates of my favourite films and TV programmes and the actor's lines that go with them. I have found a niche in public speaking which I never knew I had until late 2009 when I was preparing to speak for Autism Oxford in the New Year. I have worked with autistic students which has been a real blessing for me. My message to the people reading this book on the spectrum is that anything is possible; you just need the right foundation structure, the right people and right mind-set to prosper and flourish. That is a message to everyone on the autism spectrum.

Developmental Maturity

Mum & I in 2003 © Isaacs Family Photo

Being on the autistic spectrum from an emotional perspective I'm immature compared to neurotypical people. I would say my emotional intellect is lower (I would say I'm about 15 years old in that respect). This does affect how I cope with situations such as change and losing objects which I "need" at a specific point in time.

The biggest factor is me having alexithymia (lack of persons own self mood recognition). Statistics show that 85% of people on the autism spectrum have this within their autism.

This causes me to react late to situations of discomfort or stress which can be up to 2 weeks or 2 months! An example would be at my current workplace. During the summer holidays they changed the staff room and moved it into a bigger room in the building (so from being two smaller staff rooms it's now one massive staff room). After the summer holidays I thought I was fine about this change, but until recently I have been feeling down and anxious about this staff room. Also two members of staff who left to work elsewhere have had an effect on me but this was during the September! It has taken nearly 2 months to process this discomfort but I feel positive that I know why this is happening and what it's called.

This can cause me to be introverted and quiet and reactions to things can be heightened and immature, which shows. My parents usually know something is wrong but sometimes I can't tell them because of being alexithymic so I have to wait for my brain to process the reasons behind the emotions. However, knowledge is power and I have taken positive steps to recognise these episodes and deal with them accordingly.

An analogy I give is to imagine a very old computer that is over processing and has low disc space, and a file (a situation with an emotional input) gets downloaded on it. I consider the download my processing time and the computer to be my brain. That is how I react to things. A slow download on an old computer; I get there in the end, it just takes more time which means self-emotional recognition is an issue.

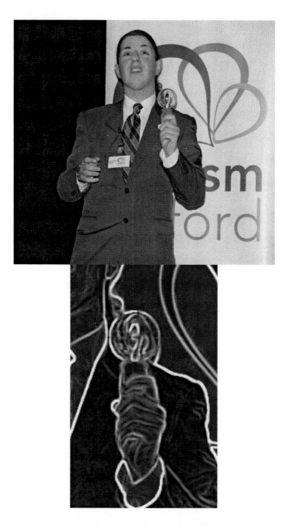

Autism Oxford Sensory Issues Event © Erangey/Isaacs

Autism

Relationships & Perceptions

For me relationships, sexual encounters and lots of friends aren't an issue. I like my autonomy; it keeps me grounded and sane. Psychiatrists and Psychologists in the field of autism still find this a rocky subject; what is the difference between AS and Autism? Some specialists believe the very difference is what the person wants out of life. People with AS want the relationships, sex & children. People with Autism do not. The other theory is that people with High Functioning Autism live in a sensory based world as opposed to a logic based world in which people with Asperger's Syndrome live in. *(Donna Williams 1995, 2005a, 2005b)* I have come to the belief that the sensory based theory is true for me although my preference is that I have never wanted nor been interested in having sexual or intimate relationships with people. I like having my friends around me and my family and that is fine for me. I'm happy and that is what counts. On a side note I consider myself Intersex which means I'm "gender neutral", both male and female (or neither depending on how you look at it). This has been very helpful to know and come to this conclusion as I feel at peace with myself.

The other difference which I have mentioned is the way in which I *perceive* the world which is in a sensory based way. For example, I have simultagnosia (object blindness), prosopagnosia (face blindness) and semantic agnosia (meaning blindness) which are a part of my autism, this meaning that I can't process surroundings, only piece by piece, and I also don't understand what the objects are within my surroundings. So I have to use my senses to work out my surrounds. When I was child I would touch, tap, lick, sniff, stare, scrape, stroke and mouth my environment to gain meaning. As I have grown I have learnt to restrict these behaviours but it comes at a price of being highly anxious and scared.

However, at home in my comfort I can simply be myself and interact with my surroundings in a way which is accustomed to my selfhood. I enjoy this time as it is a great way of dealing with the stresses of the day and a way in which I can be happy and content.

ASD & Employment

Myself Speaking at Autism Oxford Event 2011 ©
Erangy/Isaacs

There have been many times in jobs when I have found things terribly difficult. This seems to be a problem when people with ASDs want to go into employment. The problem is disclosure, employment ethos (do they understand Autism and do they have people with disabilities in their company?), getting the job and co-workers; do they understand? The questions at times seem endless. The law does state (1995 Disability Act UK) that reasonable adjustments should be made by work places to allow disabled people to work affectively. I, like many people on the spectrum, have had problems with accessing work because of lack of support, bullying, harassment (verbal) and constructive dismissals on several occasions. It has been tough but I want to be able to do things I enjoy. I started doing volunteer work in 2007/8 at a local Autism Base. This gave me real confidence and made me feel like I could be a valued member of the work force.

I went on to public speaking at Autism Oxford, a local organisation created by Kathy Erangey in late 2009 (previously called Autism Speakers & Professionals), and I value her ethos and giving me and other people on the spectrum the confidence to be supported and a valued member of society. I have been speaking for over 4 years and I enjoy it very much.

From 2011 onwards specific Autism Training was done as a part of the Autism Oxford Team as well as speaker events about specific topics and also consultancy work, I have also had experiences of working at a specialist school for people on the spectrum and provided factsheets, consultancy work and giving advice to the staff I have valued that experience. As Kathy has always said "I gave you a chance" and she is right. That's what people with Autism & Asperger's Syndrome need, a chance.

My First Job

Symbolism of my first job © Isaacs

Whatever has come my way I have always tried to take the positive out of the seemingly most negative situations, such as me being bullied out of my job after 5 years of service in which I was ridiculed by members of staff and taken advantage of. I have learned from those mistakes how certain people "ticked" in the previous workplaces and I remember it and re-direct it as knowledge for future situations of difficulty.

It does, however, make me wonder who has the problem in the context of the staff members I worked with. I tried my best; I did the work that I had to within the working day and I would try to stay away from gossip and two faced behaviours such as lying and being a braggart.

At my first job in a supermarket I did get into trouble because I was in the thick of these negative behaviours at work. I didn't understand or know how to get out of them. This caused fatigue, panic and confusion but I always tried to do my job. It took many attempts in different workplaces before I would finally be in a job where I'm accepted for me and what I can offer to the company. My message to anybody on the spectrum looking for work is never give up and always disclose your Autism to an employer because if they don't accept you for the reason that you suspect it was probably best that you should never have worked there in the first place.

ASD & Medication

The problem can be with medication and being on the autism spectrum is that it can be over prescribed or under prescribed. Being prescribed the wrong medication, which for some people on the spectrum can cause many awful side effects that have affected auto-immune system, skin, hair and mental health as a result of this, is wrong and must be tackled. Many people on the spectrum have a poor or underdeveloped immune system which causes problems with not only medication but food, drinks and the environment.

For me medication was recommended when I received my diagnosis in 2010. I think the positive situation here was that it was by a practitioner who specialised in ASDs. This made the situation much more comfortable for me, because I was very scared and anxious about taking any form of medication previously. He recommended a small dose of Citalopram (SRRI) which has been increased, by myself, until I reached a plateau of calmness. It takes the "edge" off my worries, anxieties and also helps with my OCD. I feel that I can be myself and do more in terms of productivity and performance. It has changed my life for the better.

But be warned: giving medication to younger children on the spectrum can cause damage and mental health issues and I would not recommend sorting problems with medication as a first resort.

ASD & the Internet

The internet is a massive place, a huge HUB of information and knowledge uploaded, created, designed and facilitated by people from all over the world. It is a place to share and thrive on information. However, it can be a very dark and dangerous place which can create fear and misery for people's lives.

People with ASDs have core social issues such as naivety, receptive and expressive language issues and may be more vulnerable to attack. I have sadly been on many websites and blogs that purge and spit insults about people with autism and how they are. Many of them claim that autism doesn't exist and that people who have *"mild"* autism have no real problems at all. If someone has been recently diagnosed I recommend going to safe and secure sites which have a wealth of positive and productive information. Such as the National Autistic Society which is a brilliant example of how subject related information can be compiled in a user friendly way.

ASD & "Black & White" Thinking

I have this issue myself which can cause great confusion. I can't see nor feel the "grey" of anything, like my Mum (who has got a diagnosis of Atypical Autism) she's an "*all or nothing person*" which I can relate to very much. I can achieve much within my special interests because I can be like a force of lightening and productivity! I like that feeling much like when I write books (like this one!) I get a real sense of happiness which (regardless of how long it takes to process) comes to me with arms open. I feel that people on the spectrum, regardless of where they are on the spectrum, have a right to feel and embrace happiness for their selfhood.

Communication Profile

You can't help the way you process and interpret information just like NTs have their own communication styles which differ greatly from mine and people with Asperger's. I have problems with receptive language which means I *"miss"* words people say as they're talking to me and the more detailed, monologue-like, the language is the more words I *"lose"*.

I can pick up the gurgle like "um", "hmm" and "oh" sometimes which gives me no foundation to react to what has just been said because I don't always pick up key words. This has in turn led to many misunderstandings to my reactions such as appearing non-conformist, arrogant, aloof and stupid. As a child I appeared deaf and blind because of my poor language skills, visual fragmentation and auditory distortion.

Encounters with Narcissists

I suppose the main reason for this is that people with NPD (Narcissistic Personality Disorder) tend to be socially able folks, who have a conscious awareness of manipulating others around them for their own selfish reason, such as greed, exploitation or worse. I suppose a person would be putty in their hands which they could easily exploit and use as a result of their own problems with power. I have been scared by the things that have happened to me and others by people with these characteristics. I was severely bullied and abused by female teachers at both primary school and parts of secondary school. This has left me in a state of panic when around older females because I have to *"conform"* and be a *"good boy"*, if not I will be *"punished"* and *"bullied"* as a result. No doubt these teachers had many features or even had full blown NPD as they were abusing their positions of power for the sake of a morbid fascination of making a human being unhappy. I'm sure I wasn't the first or last person to be exploited by these people but it has a lasting effect on an individual with ASD and can sometimes last for years after the event, causing panic attacks, PTSD, nightmares and flashbacks etc.

Autism & Bullying

Being true to your beliefs, positive giving and being loyal have been things that have happened in my life, such as my parents, positive values about relationships, friendships and interactions. I like to help others and feel that people have a right to be helped in times of need and so they can be confident in their abilities as a person with people on the spectrum as self-esteem can be a very big issue in the person's life.

Giving them positivity and happiness can be done in many ways because everyone is different so the approach would always be person-centred. I like to help others. It's the best thing to do. I was bullied for many reasons during my early childhood; the way I acted, the way I talked and also the way I interacted with people was "different" because of my ASD. However, in times of deep depression I was always told to just simply be true to myself. In other words I never sold out my "selfhood" for the sake of others' small minded ignorance nor their selfish natures; bullies thrive on power and, yes, there have been many times throughout my early, teenage and adult years where their behaviours have got the best of me by convincing me I was worthless and a 2nd class human being.

The truth is I always have had the positive support from my parents in these times of need and understanding they instilled positive values in me to treat people how you expect to be treated; this I try to do. Sadly others don't have this point of view. It has taken me a long time to realise that change comes from the person themselves, even bullies. One cannot change this type of behaviour if they don't see any reason to. Maybe this is because bullies get away with their behaviours on a periodic basis with a continued assault on a person.

At the age of 26 bullying still happens but I have decided to take a stand on the matter because of this repeating cycle of events from a very early age. I found that being and practicing assertiveness and taking a stand was what was needed and it worked. Taking the instilled ethos and directive nature of my parents' values on bullying I decided to voice these issues to people within the workplace. I sought advice from professionals and also joined the works union; this helped me build up a network of support so I didn't feel alone or helpless. The bullies lost this round because I decided to stand up to them and what they stood for.

Types of Bullies

In mind there are three types of Bullies

The "Psychological" Sociopath

He or she is the Bully who is *"not"* the Bully but the person reacting to your *"bad"* or *"stupid"* behaviour. They use reverse psychology and brainwashing to manipulate situations in which they have bullied a person. Like the situation of this *"former"* bully, a classic example of subtle manipulation.

- ### The "Physical" Sociopath

The Bully who uses their own physical power to dominate and subdue their *"victim"*. This can be through pushing, punching, shoving, kicking the person and making them feel worthless.

- ### The "Psycho/Physical" Sociopath

The Bully who both uses psychology and physical strength.

ASD & Selfhood

Here is an analogy I give about people respecting other people's selfhood. In the context of ASD many characteristics are sometimes intentionally or unintentionally tried to be *"removed"*, *"corrected"*, *"stamped out"*. This could be a subconscious from of conformism in which everybody has to act the same or at the very least similar. The analogy I have given in my speeches is how long would you (The NTs) last if I told you to *"Be Autistic"?* The answer was not very long because in turn it would be denying them their selfhood and characteristics. People with ASDs should be taught, within reason, to embrace themselves for who they are and all the characteristics of it.

Comfort Eating

Food © Isaacs Photo 2012

From an early age I have had a very unhealthy attitude and relationship with food. This started when I was about 7 or 8 years old, ironically when I started to gain functional speech. I would spend too much time with my Grandparents while my Mum was at work. I would eat 6–pack packets of crisps, whole packets of biscuits, cakes, ice creams etc. I had a high fat and high sugar diet for many years which was to do with mental health issues and was a way of "coping" with my problems. This isn't unique to people on the autism spectrum nor the typical spectrum. I could go further in saying it's a sad product of the westernised world and consumerism, which is partly true. This poor diet still exists today in part. I have sausage rolls and pork pies which I could live on! I like the predictable texture and taste of certain foods, hence why I keep repeating the "sensory experience" over and over again in *Groundhog Day* fashion.

Thankfully *Binge Eating* will soon be recognised as an eating disorder which is a long time coming but I'm glad that this disorder is getting not only recognition but also being able to be formally diagnosed.

ASD & Friendships

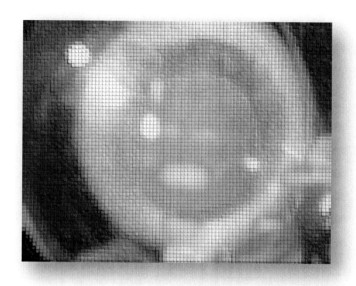

Managing friendships differently © Isaacs Photo 2012

Again, because of being Autistic rather than AS, friendships pose a different perspective for me in terms of the inter-social politics of these friendships. I have about 8 friends and enjoy their company. As a child, forming inter relationships with other people was not on my radar or agenda; my preference was always my autonomy and being alone. This wasn't because of being shunned, but rather simply the way I enjoyed myself. As I grew up the social expectations grew and in my teenage years I certainly did stand out in terms of just wanting the simplicity of having *one* friend, which was enough for me. Of course, this was frowned upon by students and teachers alike but I believe that by carrying on in that regard I wasn't selling myself out or my neurological makeup either (or course this is in retrospect but is true).

To calm down and to be at one, I need to be alone. I like to help my friends whenever I can through listening to their issues and trying to help them etc. This is something which has been exploited by many a person over the years, but I believe that those who exploit my kind nature truly have more complex problems than I do. Selfishness never gets anybody anywhere and I believe those sort of people are truly alone in the sense that they are formless and hollow. I enjoy my sense of autonomy and being alone. I don't feel bitter about it; I find it relaxing and it centres me for the day ahead and helps me *"re-fuel"* and *"recharge"*. Coping mechanisms such as stimming, playing with colourful objects, echolalia and echopraxia in some ways are my "friends" also; it makes me happy I'm not hurting anyone. Being yourself is the key to many things in life (or is it simply *the* key to life?).

I have also learned that these coping mechanisms have helped me a lot in terms of friendships and understanding others and breaking down the autistic barriers (such as trying to improve my mindblindness and differing points of view). This has helped me in social situations with my friends. I don't want loads of friends; just a cluster of decent friends around me.

I also have a strong preference for objects and things and in turn consider them friends. Also, if I'm really honest, my first friend was "water", the reason being I connected with it, enjoyed its company, its calmness and eternal beauty. I felt free and loved stimming in front of the toilet as I watched endless fragmented vision of water in front of me. So, are objects still very much part of my friendship ethos? Yes.

Experiences of Facebook

Facebook is an interesting place but bear in mind it is still cyber-land; it's not "real". It does, however, have many qualities but the problems with it are that people can defriend people for seemingly no reason whatsoever; it hurts and with no justification it can hurt badly. Maybe it's a reflection of the throwaway society we are becoming.

Just a thought: I had an incident in Facebook where I had befriended a former bully at school. I thought this person had changed. He was my friend on FB for many months, I had told him about being on the spectrum and I thought he was ok with this. I created a personal website about being on the autism spectrum and put it on his wall (bearing in mind there was no subtext going on; it was a gesture of kindness and letting him know how I was getting on in life at the moment). Minutes later he removed me as his friend. Many former students from school have removed me as friends on Facebook and I do believe it's because I have stated I'm on the spectrum. I sent him a message on Facebook asking why he did this. He commented on my poor grammar. The next message I sent was more direct and he replied by saying that I should stop living in the past (this was because I brought up about him being a bully at school).

Personally, this did upset me because I thought he had changed. But bullies always like to reverse what they're doing and this is what he did; by saying I had the problem it was taking the weight of his actions. I feel glad that in the end he showed his true colours to me and that he de-friended me. My advice to people on the spectrum is to be careful when befriending former classmates on Facebook.

Criticism - Concepts Needed

I have found that criticism is a hard one for me to take. But also it is needed - although my autistic mind may not like the idea - it's about being assertive and understanding why it's being said. From an autistic point of view this will take more time in terms of the overall picture of what is being said, how it is being said and what the reasons are behind it. Processing issues are a problem for me so going over the situation more than once certainly helps.

Backstabbing is a concept I will never understand. It's taken me years to figure out why people use this as a social tool and at 25 years old I still can't find the answer! I have been on the receiving end of many of these "backstabbing" games. It is however a form of bullying to do this and from experience in the workplace it's good to get things like this sorted out as quickly as possible through work procedure (talking to a supervisor, mentor or senior member of staff) or confronting the person yourself in a formal manner (setting up a meeting in work with the person to talk about the various issues with a witness at hand). I don't understand gossip either; in an autistic world work would be for "work" and that is it! But people forget work is a very social place and sub-text rules apply just as much as the work rules. It's good for a person to research and be given advice about these "hidden" rules in the workplace (such as gossip and backstabbing behaviours). I remember when I was 15 I thought NOBODY bullied in a workplace. How wrong I was! Positive interventions are needed so the person on the spectrum feels safe and protected in their job through understanding the FULL dynamics of the workplace.

ASD & The Importance of Emotions

Showing emotions is never a weakness; it is a part of being human to show a full variety of emotions, positive and negative, that is on spectrum of different extremes. To show being sad is nothing to be ashamed of and is just as relevant as showing that you are happy. Showing your emotions is a good thing. The key is controlling them and being able to manage difficult emotions in a socially productive manner. Sometimes it's unavoidable though. You laugh at something that to many people isn't funny (being autistic, that has happened to me many a time) and also the opposite; crying at things that you shouldn't be crying at at all.

I have been brought up by parents both of whom are on the spectrum and have shown their emotions in all their glory. I believe that this has helped me with my emotions growing up (even though I may not understand emotional build-up, because of being alexithymic, it still helps). I have no shame in showing my emotions to people I feel comfortable around, although I do find this process hard in terms of friendships. I like to try and help people in times of need and can be overly protective of them.

Humorous Account of ASD & Sex

I don't feel the need for intimate relationships with people, nor does it interest me, and I have a productive drive in my life (for reflection and processing not because of being emotionally cold, aloof or uncaring). It's not on the *"shopping list"* I suppose, and never will be. It doesn't make me sad or unhappy that I will not have a partner or children of my own. I like my life and try to embrace the good times and bad with equal positivity.

I find the thought of having sex with someone to be, quite frankly, a bore, and in my world I could find more productive things to do in that time. Which I know a lot of people will find funny. I don't mind though.

No, a cup of tea and nice hot dinner would be much more of a preference than the life of dating and having sex with many people. It's not the way I work or encounter people. I suppose there is an honesty there which I'm willing to share but this, however, doesn't mean I don't care or lookout for people who I consider my friends, but the level on which I do this is very different.

Education

The education system was a difficult time for me in terms of not understanding what I was there for. I was undiagnosed through school (I didn't receive an ASD diagnosis until 2010 at the age of 24) and school was an unhappy place for me to be in because of lack of understanding from students and staff members. To simply "be" and to be one with your "selfhood" is an enlightening experience and from that I would like to help others.

The best educational year was between 2002 and 2003 at a local college near to where I lived. It was a brilliant contrast to my previous educational years at secondary school and although I wasn't diagnosed at this point it was very much in my mind an autistic friendly environment.

It had small class sizes (5 or 6 students on the course), one to one help from the teachers, low noise levels, the correct lighting and caring and empathetic staff. This was what I consider my best educational year because many of my difficulties were being dealt with, albeit indirectly, and my grades and more importantly my happiness was greatly improved. In my view the educational system needs to implement more understanding for staff members and students in order for the person on the autism spectrum to get the same chances as the other NT peers. My other point is that knowledge of ASDs must be implemented to the whole educational system from pre-school upwards so that late or missed diagnosis will be a thing of the past; not only will it give support to the student but also to the parents as well.

Kinaesthetic Thought,

Visual Fragmentation & Monotropism

I see the pieces of things but never the wholes. My visual world is distorted as much as it is beautiful at the same time and mass of colours, lights and reflections which intrigue as much as they scare and amaze as much as they at times utterly bewilder.

I cannot piece together a physical world within my head because I'm not a visual thinker; I'm very much a kinaesthetic thinker and explorer of the world around me. This means that things have to be done in a *"mono-tracked"* way. Everything I sense has to be separated and explained to me by others because I have no filter in which to cognitively or intuitively understand where a "sound has come from" or "what I'm looking at". For example, Polytrophic (people who can multi task) don't have this issue, whereas many people on the autism spectrum are Montrophic and must do things separately. By forcing the person with autism to do something with a multi-tasking foundation can cause meltdowns.

Importance of Direction and Being Told on the Autism Spectrum

I don't understand always how I have done something right or wrong but I value being told either way so I can learn from my mistakes, which is fine, correct and necessary. It will depend on what the *rights* and *wrongs* are; if they're *judgmental rights and wrongs* then I will try to ignore them (bullying, exploiting and manipulative) but if they're directive and supportive rights and wrongs (which I value as they aren't attacking my selfhood, such as clear directions, support, exploring other options) then I will be more receptive to this because I'm not being attacked for being me but being helped within the nature of my understanding. I do, however, believe that autism is no excuse for bad manners, manipulative behaviours and using autism as an excuse for negative behaviours. It devalues and stereotypes autistic people and also takes away from the true nature of the issues which persist. I value this type of advice which I got from my parents as I was growing up.

Alexithymia & Emotions of the self

Alexithymia is a common agnosia to have within ASDs. It has a high prevalence of 85%. This is an inability to recognise one's own emotional state and relate initially to a time, place or situation. This causes me great stress when something like this happens as it has a great emotional impact on me when the emotion is negative. I have to piece together where that emotion comes from and from whom (if people were involved). It can cause me bouts of dysphoria which include fatigue, excessive crying and confusion. However, the flip side of this is when I obtain an intense positive emotion which has taken its time to process; I will have bouts of euphoria and be intensely happy and at one with my emotions.

Social Emotional Agnosia & Prosopagnosia

I try and listen to people's emotional states. Which means I rely a lot on what people tell me about themselves, as a basis and foundation of truth. I cannot read body language as it distracts me. I also have problems with recognising faces (prosopagnosia) which means that what I focus in on are the words or what the person is saying. The problem is that sometimes I only pick up on part of the conversation or a sentence of what someone is saying, denying me the interaction that was needed in order for me to understand that person's perspective. As I have grown up and been in many workplaces it came as shock to me that people lie, cheat, gossip and steal not only in the workplace but as *adults*. I had this naïve idealist view that all adults were not corrupt at all! I was in for a shock that people were deceptive and vague and didn't express their feelings because it was sometimes a very conscious thing for them to do. It still baffles me to this day that someone would deceive about such things.

Example at a work place

The only way I know how something is going on with someone in terms of their emotional state is if they explain to me how they feel inside. I have problems with body language, facial expressions and tone of voice which is called tonal agnosia. This means that I have to listen to the words (expressive) that the person is saying and process what this means. I hear words on a foundation of which they are meant. This can make life difficult and funny when you misunderstand sarcasm and jokes, but that is the nature of not picking up the "tone" or the intonation of a person's voice and what emotional input is meant by it. This means that I need time to process and understand the verbal and non-verbal messages I'm receiving from someone in order to accurately express and verbalise the correct information. I have made many mistakes but I like to learn from my mistakes.

Here is an example that happened at work (which has been paraphrased and altered):

Staff Member: *You know that person (Joe Blogs) he talks too much and goes on and on.*

Me*: Yes ok.*

Joe Blogs *walks into the corridor outside where this colleague had "exchanged" this information.*

Me*: Hi There, Mr Joe Blogs. We have just been talking about how you talk too much and go on and on.*

The social faux pas is that I saw this information on an exchange level; I have now realised that this exchange was gossip and was a product of me being "two-faced" and not telling the person, in this case Joe Blogs, what the other staff member thought of him. I thought it useful for him to know this information. He was confused and angry with me for telling him this, but to heighten that confusion he didn't seem bothered about the staff member who had told me this information.

ASD & Mindblindness

Mindblindness (Baron-Cohen 1986) is a feature of ASDs in which the person doesn't have a *"theory"* or a natural born social awareness of others' thought processes. It can cause confusion for both parties, NTs and people with ASDs, because it is an area where intentions and miscommunication is prevalent.

Interacting with the "World"

I assumed everyone was an open book. I both feared and interacted with people. I sought comfort in food and objects. I can remember being at one with all my toys (not playing with them in a typical way), feeling the ground under my feet, touching and peeling at bits of bark on trees, sniffing and playing with leaves and branches. I loved the sensory based feeling of this. I felt comfortable with shapes, colours and "*things*". Sometimes people from a visual and auditory perspective were so confusing for me that I would go mute in lessons because I wanted to leave. I would be picked on because of my language skills and unusual voice (which is like monotone).

Social Chat

I find it hard to join in conversations that have no *journey*. Small talk, gossip, point scoring conversations I find a bore and very uncomfortable. I live not to talk in times of relaxation and if I do talk it is through route echolalia (within context). My special interests, as expressed earlier in the book, are looking at various snippets of a DVD & Blu-rays which I have in my collection and playing with shiny things, coloured objects and listening to music over and over again. I only communicate when I need to with people. I also like to help people on the spectrum and the best way I can do that is by talking about their interests and it usually has to be one to one. I also like to let people with ASDs explore their interests when communication is becoming difficult.

ASD & Dissociation

I liked what could be perceived as fact or fiction but at times because of dissociation, which is a part of my autism, I would get confused about what was real and what wasn't. I would sometimes wonder if I was in a dream for long periods and have strong paradoxes of myself waking up and none of my life was real up until that point; everybody and all my things would die and disappear and I would be an older person when I woke or I would be the figment of someone else's dream or nightmare and I was never "real" in the first place. This at times used to scare me as focusing on the self was sometimes too hard so the blurring between fantasy and fiction would become more acute the more anxious I got. As of 2012 I have a recognised dissociative disorder as part of my autism.

Paul Isaacs

Other Books of Reference

Paul Isaacs' Books

© Chipmunkapublising & Paul Isaacs

- *Living Through The Haze (2012)*
- *Life Through A Kaleidoscope With James Billett (2013)*
- *A Pocket Size Practical Guide for Parents, Professionals and People on The Autistic Spectrum Foreword By Prof. Tony Attwood (2013)*

Understanding & Supporting Autistic Students in Specialised Schools (2013)

Donna Williams' Books

© Jessica Kingsley Publishers & Donna Williams

Autism: An Inside-Out Approach (1996)
The Jumbled Jigsaw (2005)

Paul Isaacs

About Author

 Paul Isaacs was thought to have severe emotional mental health problems as infant, with referrals many times in his early years, he was thought to be "developmentally underage" in his late infancy. He was non-verbal, had speech delay and gained functional speech between the ages of 7-8 years old. He was diagnosed with Autism in 2010 and Scotopic Sensitivity Syndrome in 2012 with many learning difficulties and agnosias recognised.

He currently works for Autism Oxford where he presents speeches and training around the UK to many people including professionals and people on the spectrum.

To enquire about booking Paul please contact Autism Oxford at info@autismoxford.org.uk

Paul Isaacs

Autism

Paul Isaacs

Lightning Source UK Ltd.
Milton Keynes UK
UKOW03f1939020414

229314UK00001B/56/P